40 AND PREGNANT

DAIRY OF A SECOND TIME MOTHER

SUJATHA

ISBN 979-888521520-6

This is for you

Rutvi

My Joy

Contents

Preface

Pregnancy is a wonderful phase in a woman's life. Only when one goes through it does one realize its full impact. If you are lucky enough to carry a child, cherish it. Know that you are blessed. There are many women who would love to be in your shoes.

Some people think 40 is no age to be a mother. It is not possible to get pregnant that late. It is not possible to enjoy motherhood that late.

It is possible. I was 40 years old when I conceived a second time.

Today, due to advancements in medicine and science, a 40+ woman can conceive. Her baby's health depends on her own health. If she has managed to keep herself healthy, she can give birth to a healthy baby.

Some couples have thought of having a child but have not mustered the courage to take the plunge. Some are not sure whether to go for a second child. Some are not sure whether to have a child at all.

Take the plunge. It is worth it.

There are women who are over 35 and are in a dilemma. They are not sure whether they should go for a second child and make all the adjustments – all over again. As it is, they are still trying very hard, after the first child, to put everything in place – their health, their career, their relationship. A child can disrupt everything. It is true. It does disrupt the status quo.

But it is worth it!

I repeat that.

The Beginning

CHAPTER I

Why? Why Not?

Why should you opt to have a child?

I opted to have my first child for two reasons.

One was practical. I became pregnant without trying. The journey of the egg and the sperm coming together to create a beautiful life is nothing short of a miracle. It is one of the most mysterious and magical journeys of the universe.

Watch videos on the internet to appreciate the beauty and splendor of the process of conception. You will know what I mean.

You cannot buy this experience. No matter how much money you have, or how many degrees you have earned, or how long you have tried to be pregnant, or how many medical treatments you have undergone to conceive, you cannot be a (biological) mother unless God wishes you to be and at the time He wishes it to happen. It is entirely in God's hands.

So, if I got pregnant without trying for it, I felt I should go on the whole journey. I was grateful to the universe for this miracle that happened in my womb.

The other reason why I went for my first child was sentimental. I wanted to experience motherhood firsthand. I wanted to experience everything - from the conception to the nine months of the pregnancy to the labor and the delivery.This is an experience that is reserved only for women. In my next life, if I am born a man, I will miss out on it.

That is why I had Tanvi, my first daughter.

Why Not?

I did not want to have a second child.

The reason?

Because I had already gone through the entire experience once. I had seen it all. I had been there and done that. Why would I want to repeat the same experience again?

I know of people who did not have a great experience during their first pregnancy, delivery, and subsequent childrearing. That bitterness is now stopping them from going for a second child.

I was one of them!

With Tanvi, I had done it; that too all alone, single-handedly. I knew how horrifyingly lonely it gets sometimes and how terribly painful some days are. I did not want to go through it again. Why would I, in my sane mind, want to suffer the hell of labor pain, the nine months of captivity, the stress of raising a baby, the countless hours, days and nights of wanting to kill myself because I was so damn tired? Why would I want to go for it again? Once was enough; more than enough.

Many women do not go for a second child because they do not have access to good child-care facility around them. They do not have any child support system at home either – no parents, no in-laws. In situations like these, it is natural to feel that a second child means trouble.

It definitely is a lot of trouble.

No doubt about it.

CHAPTER II

The Realization And The Alarm Bell

Having a second child is worth all the trouble.

Today, after having my own second child, I can say that with complete honesty and confidence.

So then, what is the right reason to have a second child?

When Tanvi was very young, sometimes I would find her feeling lonely. I would see her smothering other kids and babies with love. Whether the child was older or younger than her, age did not matter to her. I felt she was missing the companionship of a sibling in her life. She longed for company. When she had someone to play with, she was happy to be with the kid for hours and days together.

I played with her too, but it was not the same. Two children playing together and a child and adult playing together is very different.

She would often play by herself. She would ingenuously role-play - talk to a water tap on the terrace, or the chair or the sofa in the hall or the railing of the stairway. She would pretend these things were people. She would have a conversation with them.

I would watch all that and feel bad. I would feel momentarily miserable that she did not have a sibling to play with. Or even a kid in the building or the neighborhood. I wanted to give her a friend, a lifelong friend. Not the kind who come and go on weekends.

Among the neighborhood children, the big ones bullied her. The little babies would only coo along. They were always under a 24 hours surveillance of their parents. So, if Tanvi so much as bent over to plant a kiss on the baby's cheeks, the parents would shriek "NO".

They would forget that Tanvi was only four years old, a baby herself. They would expect her to be all sacrificing with her toys and crayons and cars. Even if the other baby hit her hard, they would expect Tanvi to not hit back as a reflex action.

At those times, I so wanted to give her a sibling who she could talk to and play with.

Some women go for a second child because their mother-in-law or husband asked them to. Some opt for two kids as it is a 'must' for a family. Some feel the second child ensures that should something happen to one of them, you will still have one more to hold on to. If one dies, you have the other to carry on the family name. This is particularly true if you cross the child-bearing age.

I feel the only good enough reason to have another child is if you want to enjoy the joys of motherhood one more time. Pregnancy and raising a child are a roller-coaster ride. Nothing else can help you sail through that ride than the conviction that you really wanted this.

You wanted to experience the happiness one last time.

The Alarm Bell

17th June 2017 was our 12th wedding anniversary.

That whole week, I was feeling very uncomfortable.

My stomach felt bloated. It was like something was "IN" there. I wanted to burp loudly so it could come out and free me of my discomfort.

In just a week, I had drunk three bottles of different soft drinks. This by itself was unusual. I don't drink soft drinks at all. I don't enjoy it much. I always go for milkshakes and sometimes just take a sip if Tanvi offers her glass of Coke.

But I had drunk three bottles in a week. I was so desperate to burp and release the gaseous feeling. Three bottles in a week was the first alarm bell.

Two days later, as I sat with that "something in my stomach" feeling, I casually remarked to Sathya, my husband, that maybe I am pregnant. I searched for “the early signs of pregnancy” on my phone. It had symptoms like fatigue, nausea, constipation, mood swings and so on. I had been feeling all this.

But since I didn’t know any better, I had attributed it to indigestion.

I asked Sathya to get me the home pregnancy kit to check if I was right.

Tanvi and he stared at me.

They had an expression of utter disbelief.

CHAPTER III

The News And The Moment Of Truth

I woke up the next day at my usual time - 6 a.m. I took the test. My result was in my hands.

For some inexplicable reason, I remembered the episode from "*Friends*" where Rachael takes the test. Phoebe and Monica tell her the result is negative. Rachael is, surprisingly, disappointed. She had been wanting, unknown even to her, the result to be positive.

I woke up both Sathya and Tanvi, much before their usual time and broke the news to them. I showed them the two lines. I was pregnant!

For an hour after that, we all lay on the bed talking about it and wondering what to do next. I forgot that Tanvi had school and she would be late. We hugged each other and stared at the two lines!

Strangely, Tanvi was eager to have the baby. All these years, it was she who had vehemently told us not to have another baby. It was both strange but nice to hear her talk of wanting a sibling.

The test result was the second surprise of the day.

The first was the realization that I had gotten pregnant a second time. I had conceived, once again, without trying for it. I was pregnant once again after eleven long years.

The Moment of Truth

Sathya did not want to keep the baby. He said, “Let’s remove it." He had said the same words last time as well. It had become his standard line.

Later that day, we planned to go to the doctor to confirm the pregnancy. Tanvi went to school, happy in the thought that, we would bring her the news that even the doctor confirmed the pregnancy.

But we didn't go to the doctor that day.

We went to Taj Biryani restaurant in Shivajinagar because Sathya was craving for their biryani. I was pregnant and he was craving! It was Ramzan. There were no customers in the restaurant. I couldn't eat the biryani. It tasted too sour to me.

The following morning, I went for a walk in the park adjacent to our house. Sathya accompanied me. The plan was to go to the doctor later in the day and remove the fetus. I begged him to change his mind. But he told me it was not practical to have the baby. Just a few days back, I had accepted a new job as Deputy Manager – Training. It was an excellent opportunity both in terms of pay and career growth. In a week's time, I was confirmed to join them and start work. It was an 'either this or that' situation. I could either have the baby or the job. Not both.

Our ages, me 40 and he 36, was also a factor. Why would we go through the whole childbearing and childrearing process once again?

He also added, "Look at my salt and pepper beard. Is it a time for one more baby?" I imagined this giant 6 feet 3 inches, 126 kilo man running behind a toddler. He was right. This was no time for one more baby.

But there was a part of me that was disturbed. I needed to speak to someone.

I messaged Sapna, a school friend and doctor in Australia. I also messaged Suzaan in Kuwait and Asha in Switzerland. Three friends, in three different countries, and three perspectives. I needed more voices. And they were all well-meaning friends. I had not met them after school, not even once. But somehow, sometimes, people far away from you, seem to be so close.

Sapna gave me a holistic view. Pregnancy was not just an emotional decision but also a medical one. It was a very balanced advice. Suzaan instilled hope that this could be a new direction and new motivation of life. Asha, who was herself a mother of three boys, was sure that we must keep the baby. The conversation with them was making things clearer to me. It was helping me become aware of what I really wanted.

Meanwhile, Sathya stuck to his 'remove it' stand and went to the salon to cut his hair. I called up Babu, his childhood friend and told him about the pregnancy. There was no one else I knew who could convince him. Also, there was no one, among his friends, I was comfortable enough to talk to about such a delicate matter. I urged him to do it soon. In less than two hours, we would be in the maternity clinic. At ten, we had planned to go to the doctor for the abortion. Babu said he will speak.

And he did - for half an hour - even as the barber was busy massaging Sathya's head. He called me back saying "Good news, Sathya will be distributing sweets today". Sathya agreed to keep the baby.

While I was in the shower, Sathya returned from the salon. I heard the TV. I came out thinking he would lift me up and scream with joy, "Wow! I am going to be a father again." I had always wanted that filmi scene where the heroine does this whole coy thing, twirling the edges of her saree and the hero lifts the heroine and shouts "I am going to be a father" and does an impromptu dance.

Instead, Sathya asked me, "What did you do? You had agreed yesterday to remove and now you are saying no. What if we had removed it yesterday itself?" I sighed. No filmi scene for me!

CHAPTER IV

Why At 40?

Why now? Why so late? That was the first question the screening doctor asked me when I went for my first check-up.

And then the others - acquaintances, neighbors, friends – had the same question too.

But the question Sathya and I had was: HOW? How did it happen?

We were married for twelve years. We were rarely rolling under the sheets. I thought I was nearing menopause. So, even if we went under the sheets on rare occasions, I was sure I could not or would not become pregnant. Such naivete at 40!

I seriously never thought it was possible for me to get pregnant anymore.

But one day, one session and one sperm runs right across and meets the egg, says hello and BAM - sets the ball rolling. Literally.

So, my honest-to-God answer to the question 'Why' is that, in my case, it was an accident. It just happened. We never planned it. We never consciously wanted it. It was completely unexpected and in equal measures, shocking and exhilarating.

Now that it had happened, we went for it.The thought of abortion disturbed me. I could not get myself to abort the baby.

I could not get myself to kill a life breathing inside me.

This meant I had to kill my career. I had to let to go of the opportunity. Job would have to wait.

The 'When' Question

After 'how', the next question on our minds was 'when'. When did I conceive? We were still surprised that I had conceived after all these years.

When I became pregnant with Tanvi, it was easy to guess the 'when'. We were just three months into our marriage when we came to know I had conceived. We were wild and young and madly in love and crazily physically attracted to each other. So, with her conception, 'when' was never a question. There were hundreds of instances!

But this time around, we were puzzled. I had Tanvi in 2006 and had started using IUCD immediately after. I used it for ten years from 2006 to 2016. I did not get pregnant during the ten year period.

I had removed the IUCD in June 2016. So, the conception happened between 2016 and 2017. It had taken just a few occasional moments of intimacy and removal of IUCD for the miracle to happen.

If the baby was one month old, it must have happened sometime in May. But now, 'when' in May? Let's funnel down.

In the last week of April and first week of May, we were at his parents' house in RR Nagar as it was school vacation for Tanvi. When a couple is into their twelfth year of marriage, they know very well how infrequent their romp sessions are.

We could easily pinpoint the day of the rendezvous in our case. It happened on the 5th of May! Tanvi had gone swimming that day. The others in the house were taking their afternoon nap.

We had not indulged in another session till the end of May when we were in Paradise Isle in Malpe.

Voila! We zeroed in on the exact day! We were professional solvers of conception mysteries!

The First Visit

We went to Dr. Rao in L.M. Maternity Clinic, Malleshwaram. It was the same hospital where I had delivered Tanvi.

Interestingly, Dr.Rao had delivered Sathya in 1980. And then his first daughter in 2006. And now his second baby in 2018.

We people from Dakshin Kannada have this implicit faith in people of our own region. Whether it is medicine, food, or any other service, we blindly trust each other's expertise. We are assured of good quality service. We also know we won't be robbed of our hard-earned money. How much of it is statistically true - I can never be too sure. But, in my case, it has been true.

The screening doctor did the preliminary question-answer round. When I said I am 40, she immediately retorted, "Why did you delay your second pregnancy so much? There are high chances of Down's Syndrome."

In all the excitement of the new baby and the sadness of not taking up the new job, I completely missed this. I never thought of it! My heart skipped a beat.The doctor's voice was scary and discouraging. I felt disheartened. I told Sathya about the warning. He got angry and said, "Tell her to f**k off."

The seed of doubt had been sown in my mind. I feared the possibility.

Dr. Rao was as cheerful as she was a decade ago, during my first pregnancy. She asked if we were planning to keep the baby. She was happy with the affirmation. I was prescribed Folic acid tablets for the next three months.

I came home and searched YouTube for what folic acid did and realized the tiny tablets were important for forming what is called the neural tube of the baby. I kept watching the video again and again. The fertilized egg repeatedly dividing into smaller, individual cells, each cell later forming an organ, the spinal shape, and the elongation of the embryo - fascinating.

The Due Date

I got the expected due date (EDD) for the delivery of the baby. It was 9th of February. The baby will be an Aquarian, like me! I started my calculations.

If the baby is born **AFTER** the EDD:

If the baby is born ten days later, he will be born exactly on MY birthday. Yay! Mother and baby same birthday.

If the baby is born five days later, he will be born on Valentine's Day. Still, Yay!

If the baby is born **BEFORE** the EDD:

If the baby is born two days before, he will be born on my mother's birthday. Yay! He will be a very kind person, just like my mother.

If the baby is born three days before, he will share the birth number with big sister Tanvi. Both born on 6th of the month.

If the baby is born seven days before, he will have a unique Date of Birth. 02-02! Born on the second day of the second month of the year. Big sister Tanvi's DOB is very special too - 06.06.06!

If the baby is born **WAY** before, he will be born on Republic day.

Had I done all permutations and combinations of possible birth dates? I think I had.

The First Trimester

CHAPTER V

The Scans

I was two months pregnant. It was time for the first scan. The baby already had a silhouette! The doctor wanted us to go for specific tests to negate the possibility of Down's Syndrome.

At three months, we had the Nuchal Translucency scan. We saw the baby's position and shape. The baby showed good leg and hand movements. We saw the heart and the in & out movement of the blood flow.

I love hearing the heartbeat of babies. It is so loud and fast.

The doctor said the baby is six centimeters now. I was perplexed "That's it? Six centimeters? All that trouble of the first three months for just six centimeters?!"

One day, Sathya said he had a beautiful dream. The baby boy was healthy and round and had not cried and had big open eyes looking around and the doctor gave him the baby to hold. "The baby was staring with his big eyes" he said.

We both would like to have a boy this time just so that we have one of each gender. I want to raise a son, the way a son should be raised – taught to do household chores and helping in the kitchen like we expect our daughters to do. I wanted to be a revolutionary mom. Someone who teaches her son to clean and keep house. I wanted to the raise a son who treated a woman as an equal and didn't feel entitled.

CHAPTER VI

Comfort Food And Nausea

During the entire first trimester, I had not eaten mutton or chicken, not even fish. I had turned almost 100% vegetarian!

I remember immediately after I turned 40 in February, I had wanted to give up on meat. And now, it had happened, quite organically. I didn't even know when I stopped eating or liking it much. Now, I just love the smell of dal and sabzi. I spend two hours cooking. And I eat almost as soon as the lunch is ready. And as soon as I am done eating, within half an hour, I sleep peacefully for an hour or two. Absolute bliss!

My comfort food was idli. Two idlis with sambar – hunger successfully squashed. Fermented food is healthy. Also, idli is a safe bet. Every other snack varies in taste from restaurant to restaurant. One can't be sure. But idli tastes the same in every restaurant whether price is Rs 5 or Rs 15. May be softer in some restaurants but basic taste doesn't differ much. So, no risk of buying and not liking it and being forced to change the order and having to eat something else. Idli with sambar is tasty, light, healthy and easily available anytime, anywhere.

I had a strong craving for sweets. I used to make at least one sweet everyday – kheer, sheera and so on. I was craving for sugar, a lot!

This time, as I was not working and was at home, I was conscious of the slightest discomfort. When you are working, your mind is pre-occupied with a million other things.

I was hungry all the time. Every three hours I ate something. I had to. Otherwise, I felt this biting, slicing pain. Luckily, since I was not working and I had so much time on hand, I had developed a never-before-felt love for cooking!

Yes, I had started enjoying my time in the kitchen!

When I was pregnant with Tanvi, I used to order Malleshwaram Hallimane meals for lunch every single day in the office. It cost eighteen rupees back in 2005. I ate that throughout her pregnancy. Long live Hallimane! They are from Dakshin Kannada too. See, we always find our own!

These past three months, I have spent a lot of time cooking. YouTube videos are a Godsend. I start cooking at 11 and finish by 1. I make one curry, one vegetable side-dish, and rice. Some days, I take hot lunch for Tanvi to her school which is four minutes' walk from our house. As soon as I am done cooking, I hear the loud rumbles from my tummy and I immediately attack my plate. Hot, tasty, homemade lunch slipping down your food pipe – heaven! Now I know, why we Hindus consider 'Anna' as 'Brahma' (Food is God).

I made semolina sweet. It turned out ok. No one else ate. I had to eat it alone. I made vanilla ice cream cake bread. It flopped big time. I made bhindi rava fry. It was a success. I made cucumber curry mangalore style. It was a super success. I made aloo paratha. It was a super success. I made moong dal halwa. It was a flop. I made cauliflower side-dish. It was a success.

I made Marie biscuit cake. It was a success. But Tanvi and Sathya did not eat it. They said, "Can't you just eat Marie biscuits? What is all this cake nonsense? It smells and tastes of Marie from a kilometer away." But it was a hit in Tanvi's school. I had sent four big pieces and her friends devoured it.

I made radish side-dish once. It turned like how they serve in Hindu functions. Radish was not a vegetable on my radar before that! I also made Vangibath powder. It is a breakfast item made with those long, thin, green brinjals.

I have also introduced myself to dill leaves! I made dill leaves parathas. Both Tanvi and Sathya not only ate it but asked for more which is the ISI mark for saying it was good. I once made Malabar spinach curry. I once made the North Karnataka style brinjal gravy. I had put 6 brinjals in it and since both Tan and I don't eat brinjals, Sathya had to eat them all!

Nowadays, Tanvi's lunch box is a much sought after one in her class. Her friends love what I cook and even make demands saying, "Ask your mother to make that ladies finger semolina fry again."

Nausea

Nausea is common during pregnancy. Watch any Indian movie where the heroine is married or raped, there will be a scene where she runs to the backyard and pukes. That alerts the audience to the next scene – either a scene of happy celebration or a scene of wholesale shaming of the woman.

I had vomited only twice in the past three months. The nausea is always there, though. It reduced considerably over the next few weeks. I remember, the second time I vomited, I was already in the shower. Tanvi came running with a glass of water. I was sitting there with my head in my hands. It completely drains you of every ounce of energy. I came out and plonked on the bed.

And then, you suddenly realize that your man hasn't lifted his eyes off his phone even as you were puking to death. That's when you muster all your strength and throw the first curse of the pregnancy at your man – "*May he be born a woman in his next life and may he puke every single day of his first trimester!*"

IUCD

I was 49 kilos at the start of my first pregnancy in 2006. I was 28 years old then. I was 63 kilos at full term. I had shed the pregnancy weight of Tanvi within a couple of months. I was back at 55 without any diet or gym or any exercise. I breast fed her for three years.

I am 40 now. I am at 59 kilos at the start of my second pregnancy in 2017. I dread to think what I will peak at. 75 kilos? How am I going to carry myself?

Many say if we are on IUCD, it makes you put on weight. Nothing of the sort happened to me. In fact, there never ever was any pain or the slightest discomfort. Five years of protection for under Rs 3000. IUCD is the most economical, stress free and comfortable family planning option. Insert and forget!

In 2011, I had gone to Mudbidri to meet Lizzy, my friend and senior in Mangalore University. During a conversation, she casually mentioned that we need to remove it past its expiry date. The expiry date is five years. THAT reminded me about my IUCD! I had forgotten about it. As soon as I returned to Bangalore, I hurried home to check what the expiry date was on mine. I had crossed two months past the date! I ran to the doctor the very next day, removed the first one and got the second one inserted. Thank God for that talk with her!

CHAPTER VII

Highs and Lows

Extreme emotional highs and lows during pregnancy is a real thing. I was in a perpetually lousy mood, especially during the first trimester and could fly off the handle at the slightest provocation.

I remember one incident. Two days before the start of Tanvi's school, we went to Malpe beach. Sathya and I got into an argument in the car regarding the music and the volume. And we fought.

One topic led to another. Women can bring up totally bizarre past records into a current fight. I did it too. I am beginning to think I am an expert in raking up past grievances. I have like a special storage space in my brain set aside for keeping track of all old humiliations.

Exasperated, he said "Let's separate."

This was the first time ever that he had said it in the past twelve years. I say it once a year. That's my most potent threat since I don't have the luxury that other women have. Other women can say "I will go to my mother's house".

He had never ever uttered that word. And now he did. I was shocked. I thought maybe I should delete or burn that storage space inside my damn brain. Out loud, I only said 'OK', turned around on the seat and pretended to sleep. This was end of May and I was already three weeks pregnant by then but of course I didn't know it.

It is strange now, to think of that fight and how, even as we talked of going our separate ways, there was a new life growing within me to keep us together. At the Shimoga hotel where we stayed the night, Tanvi overheard us talking of separating. I hugged her as we slept and told her, "We will be living separately and from now on you will have 2 of everything – two houses, two birthdays and two gifts".

She wrapped her arms and legs around me and started weeping. She just wouldn't hear another word. She was inconsolable. She kept saying 'NO! I want BOTH". I thought I heard Sathya sobbing softly in the adjacent bed. He had uttered those words in anger, and he couldn't take them back now. He didn't mean it, but it was too late.

I never knew how physically strong Tanvi was and how deeply attached she was to the idea of the three of us as one family unit, until that night. She hugged me so tightly that it hurt me. All three of us cried ourselves to sleep that night.

I think divorce affects children in ways that we adults can never imagine. They always want both parents with them.

Tanvi was conceived just three months after our wedding. I had literally jumped into this marriage. Just 3 months of courtship and we were married. He was 25 years old at the time, reckless, and irresponsible. I was at a new job, new relationship, new house, and new family. His parents didn't even sleep in the direction of our house; such was his mother's animosity towards me. Reason for her animosity, you ask. According to her, I wasn't beautiful enough for her "Star" Son.

I contemplated many times to end the whole ordeal. It was a marriage that was giving heartache to everyone involved. It was pointless to waste precious human life, his and mine, in such a futile union.

But who knew that Tanvi, who was growing within me at the time, was coming to keep us together?

Once again, I am two heartbeats. There is another tiny heart beating along with mine, stronger and harder.

Sometimes that knowledge is so humbling and gratifying. Another life within me! A heart that is pumping furiously! And sometimes, the thought is plain bothersome, especially when you must constantly go to the loo to pee.

There is no induction training or trial sessions or demos for pregnancy. At least back then, I didn't attend any prenatal classes or watch any YouTube videos. Now, thanks to smart phones and internet, everything, every information is available on your fingertips. And today, the second time around, I have watched many a video and read countless pregnancy related articles.

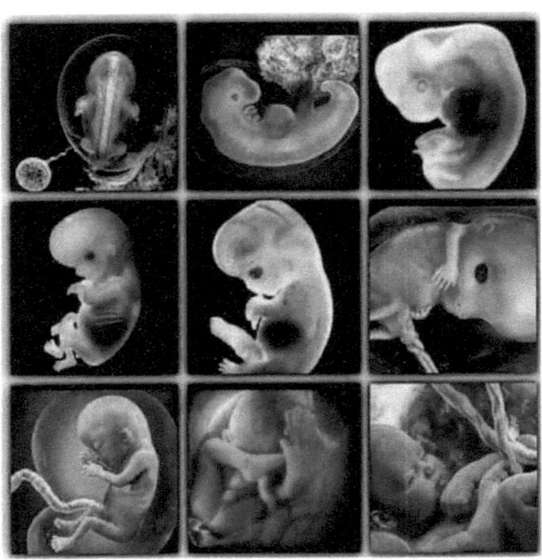

CHAPTER VIII

Down's Syndrome

The doctors kept saying there are chances that my baby would have Down's Syndrome. It troubled me.

I came home and watched You Tube videos on Down's Syndrome. The videos were heart-wrenching. I was devastated.

I had to constantly reassure myself that just because I was 40 and medical science says the chances of Down's Syndrome increases with the increase in the maternal age, it didn't mean that my baby would have it.

No, my baby is not going to have it. I will not worry. I am going to deliver a healthy baby. I had already done it once. I had delivered a healthy Tanvi. When I had delivered her, it was not in the best of the circumstances. I was a train-wreak both physically and emotionally. This time, I was resting, cooking all my meals, not eating out at all, eating every three hours. Things would be fine.

It is unbelievable that so many scans need to be done if the mother's age is above 35. The father could be an 80-year-old man. It doesn't matter.

As the fetus grows in the mother's body, HER age is what matters. With Tanvi, since I was 28, there were hardly any scans that needed to be done. This time, one after the other, the dreaded 'S' word. It was terrifying to hear the doctor say that word.

If you are planning to have two kids: plan the second one well before you hit 34. That way, there will not be any worries about so many scans and blood tests. You will not be under pressure to do tests just to see if there are any defects in the growing fetus due to your age.

Babies are emotional decisions for parents. It is natural to forget the money angle in our excitement of parenthood.

The truth is babies are expensive. Scans don't come cheap. It starts at Rs 1000. Blood tests start at Rs 600. Your vitamins and minerals cost a minimum of Rs 400 a week. Doctor consultation starts at Rs 300. We have already spent close to Rs 7,000 for three of these in three months of check-up. And that is just for the scans and blood tests. It is excluding medicines, consultation fees, trips to the clinic. This is even before the baby is born.

Once it is born, the cost just skyrockets. It's nice to cuddle and coo-coo to a baby that giggles when it sees you but without proper care, which also means money, in addition to love, things can get bumpy.

So, if you are serious about adding a second member to your family, plan it! Make sure you, the mother, conceive before you hit 34. Save money.

The Second Trimester

CHAPTER IX

Flashback

Now that I had entered the fourth month, the energy had returned. I felt less drowsy. In the first trimester, I used to sleep a minimum of twelve hours every day, eight hours at night and four hours during the day. That was almost half a day spent sleeping.

I had been sleeping a lot less now and that too not the earlier 'lost in a deep, deep slumber' kind of sleep. Sometimes, I did not even sleep in the mornings, though the afternoon nap time continued.

I had not eaten a single morsel of any sweet. I don't crave for it anymore. I prefer my regular, slightly spicy food.

I could not see the tiny, side bone on my ankle anymore. It was buried under all the new fat. Toes were visibly plump. I had to remove my

toe-rings. I had already given away a big bag of clothes that I could not fit into anymore. And ordered my first 'nighty' from Amazon.

I wanted to start walking. I had not walked since I got pregnant and I had not walked even before that. I must start. I did not want a C section.

June-July the weather was so cold, and breezy I couldn't step out even with a sweater on. I was shuddering. Now in August, the weather had warmed up. I was sleeping with the fan speed at five which is saying a lot and yet I had not started walking.

Walking had made my last delivery easy. Even though it was just walking from home to office, from 8th Cross to 6th Cross, Malleshwaram, less than 2 kms daily, it still helped. Tanvi's was a two-hour labor and relatively smooth. She had turned her head a week before the delivery and everything went well.

I remember the day I delivered her. The water had broken around 10 a.m in the morning and by 12 I had been admitted.

By 2 the contractions started and by 4 p.m my baby was in my arms.

No wait, she wasn't.

She was not in my arms because after the delivery, I had fallen asleep. Or I fell unconscious. Or the doctor had put me to sleep with painkillers. I don't know exactly.

Childbirth is very painful. Research says that it is rated 10/10 on the pain scale. It is a pain that is one of a kind. It is experienced only by one-third of the population.

For some women, the contractions hurt more than the pushing. Some women feel the pain is like menstrual cramps. It starts off as a heavy menstrual cramp and gets worse with time. The contractions can be more painful as they last for hours together. This is because your entire body below the ribs is constantly working on bringing that little on into the world through your vaginal cavity. It takes really long for your baby to prepare for birth as the contractions keep coming and hitting your body like a wave of pain. Pushing on the other hand takes a lot less you don't find it so painful.

For others, the final push almost made them pass out due to the excruciating pain. Remember how you scream in pain after stubbing your little toe on the table's edge? That hurt brings tears to your eyes and you abuse the little corner. If that little stub can knock the living daylights out of you, what about childbirth then?

All I can recollect now is that they had moved me, from the delivery area to an adjacent area, to be shifted to a ward as soon as it was available.

All wards were full that day.

There really are a lot of Gemini kids in the world. I read somewhere that Gemini is the most common zodiac and Aquarius is the rarest. There are far too many Geminis in this world and far few Aquarians. September must be a great month for conception and May the worst month. Something to do with the cooler/warmer weather in those months?

Anyways, I remember seeing, in my drowsy state and droopy eyes, the nurse showing the baby to Sathya. And then, my eyes closed. When I woke up, I was in a ward with tiny Tanvi next to me - all of 2.92 kg.

It was a common ward, the only one available, so there were 2-3 other mothers as well. A nurse asked me if I had fed the baby. I had not. I didn't know I had to!! I didn't know what to say to the nurse. I was afraid she would shout at me. I hadn't even lifted my baby in my arms yet. I was completely drained of energy. I had apparently passed out for a good 3-4 hours and the baby hadn't had anything yet. So, I slowly raised myself on the bed, took the baby and ... sat.

I didn't know what to do next.

Who gets a lesson in feeding? It is like sex. You don't know it until you do it. It is instinct, by and large. Or if your mother or mother-in-law is next to you, she guides you. My great mother-in-law was too busy handling matters of World Peace to be beside me. She had not turned up at all, even that late in the day, to see her grandchild. So, well, I too followed my instinct. And boy, was Tanvi hungry!

That first moment when you feed your baby is a moment a woman will never forget in her life. That is when the two of you "connect" and "bond" and watching those tiny lips on your bosom, you finally feel that yes, it was all worth it. The struggles of the nine months, the pain of labor, the delivery trauma - all worth it. I know people say, the moment immediately after delivery, is the greatest - the moment when you see your baby for the first time. But for me, that moment was fleeting. The doctor was busy stitching me up, giving instructions to 'hold up' my legs so that she could have a better view and control while she stitched and finishing up the rest of the post-delivery tasks. The baby was not given to be held because it had to be washed and was not laid next to me because I had passed out. What they show you in the movies, it doesn't always work that way.

After I had fed her on one side, I thought it's not fair to feed only one side. I must be impartial (typical teacher talk) and feed both. Someone later told me that yes, that is the right way to do it; otherwise the breast swells and hurts like hell because the milk coagulates. Always feed both sides.

I had read that breast-feeding is equivalent to running eight kilometers. I had breast-fed Tanvi till she was three years old. I fed her everywhere – theater, cinema hall, bus-station. I fed her on everything –bus, car, bike, auto. I now believe it was one of the reasons I lost all the pregnancy weight (thirteen kilos) so quickly and that too without any exercise or any fitness regime.

CHAPTER X

Dreams

I had completed four months. Sathya had another dream. He saw a plump baby trying to stand but could not stand. The baby was also trying to sit but kept falling backwards. He had this sweet smile as he woke up in the morning, lay on the bed and narrated the dream. It felt nice to have a man, whose first words were, "Let's remove it", dream of his baby and talk about it with such fondness in his voice. Gratifying. I did not have these precious moments when I was pregnant with Tanvi. So, these little things are heart-warming.

I hadn't heard of any dreams the first time around with Tanvi. So yeah it warmed my heart to hear about it this time. I guess God really heard my prayer. I must have called out to him loudly and piously or as they say, if you pray for something with all your heart, the whole universe conspires to give that to you.

I had prayed fervently to have a happy, pleasant pregnancy experience. The first one was full of strife – external I mean. I was working hard at a new job, Sathya wasn't yet responsible, I had to manage home, office, him, AND the pregnancy. We were going to discos and pubs with his friends almost every evening. Throughout those 9 months, I don't remember sleeping during the day or during holidays or ever taking rest.

I remember my dreams were full of food last time. I was underfed and hungry. I craved for food during all my waking hours. This time, I had not dreamt of food even once. I enjoyed every little morsel that I ate even if it was something as simple as a boiled egg. Everything tasted good and I had not said no to anything. I was thankful for this. I truly was. Most pregnant women don't realize the value of food because they are pampered silly during all their pregnancies. They do not know what 'not having' means. They do not know what 'longing for' and 'thinking about food all the time' means. But I know! I have been through it. And today, it makes me so grateful for every plate that I have relished and polished off. And I hope it stays that way.

I got a dream today. I saw a premature but fully grown baby. Then Tanvi brought a tiny baby from the washroom!! That turned out to be my real baby. Like always, I googled for meaning of the dream. It said I am not ready for the future.

Can pregnant ladies be not ready? I guess we can. Most of us do go through fleeting moments of self-doubt, and self-questioning. Sometimes, I stare at my tummy and wonder, "Is this real? Is it really happening? I can see the bulge but is there really a human in there who will come out one day?"

CHAPTER XI

The Breakdown

In the fourth month check-up, the report of the Quadruple test was negative. Everything was normal, no defects. The odds of me having a Down Syndrome baby were down to 1:384.

But then, the doctor suggested another scan to check chances of Down Syndrome. AGAIN! In three visits, three scans recommended. First it was the blood test and the first trimester scan, then it was double-marker test (which we couldn't do as we went two weeks late) and so did Quadruple test and now one more - Anamoly scan.

I don't know what hit me, but I broke down and started crying. I told Dr. Leela Rao that every time I come for check-up, I am asked for some defects-detection test, just because I am 40. She said it is only to ensure the baby is healthy and that I have come for only three check-ups. I asked her what if one of the tests came out positive. What then? She said then we will have to abort the baby.

I knew the answer.

I guess I wanted to hear it out loud.

My heart sank.

She then asked me not to worry. All these scans are precautionary measures only. Everything is in the hands of God. She herself was the twelfth child and her mother delivered her at the age of 45! "Plus", she added, "You have a God-fearing husband. Believe in God. Everything will be fine."

When we came out of the clinic, I had resigned myself to my fate. I am 40, my chances of having a Down

Syndrome baby are high. I must accept and go through all the scans, without tears or remorse.

It was time for the dreaded Anamoly Scan and fifth month check-up. There was also blood and urine test. I was made to drink two glasses of glucose and after two hours, the blood and urine samples were taken.

The scan this time was to check if all the functions of the growing baby were normal. And it was. We saw the lips, nose, brain, heart, and kidneys of the baby. The stomach area was filled with fluid which means the kidneys were working fine. The brain was surrounded by a fluid which is also a good sign. The scan went on for thirty minutes.The baby had clenched its fist the first time the assistant scanned. Later, after an hour, when the doctor did the scan again, she pressed the abdomen slightly harder and the baby opened its fists slightly.

In the first trimester scan, the visuals were clearer. We could see the entire baby. This time, it was sort of blurred and we couldn't see the complete body. The baby had grown, and they could not show the full body. The focus was on examining each organ in detail. The backbone of the baby looked just like fish bone. No cleft lips, the lips looked fine.

My risk for birth defects had come further down - from 1.38 to 1.76. That's good news. Next month check-up would be a regular one – checking blood pressure, weight etc. No scan. Thank God.

Sathya was trying to see the genitals. We had read that by fifth month, if it is a boy, the genitals would be formed and would have dropped down and would be discernible. We could not see anything.

Strangely, I never felt to eat raw mango even once during these six months. In fact, I did not feel so even in Tanvi's pregnancy. A pregnant woman craving for raw mango must be one of those movie cliches.

This picture was taken last month when I had already completed five months and was rushing towards the sixth month. On that evening, the jerks were more pronounced. We could even "see" the skin on the tummy moving. Tanvi was constantly talking to the baby, tapping, and tickling to elicit more kicks.

I had completed twenty-three weeks. I had gained two kilos in the past one month; out which half a kilo is the weight of the baby. I was at sixty kilos now and the back pain was pronounced. I had started feeling the jerks of the baby. Could not say they were kicks or movements, not just yet. But I was conscious of slight jerks and twitches. I had made Tanvi feel it too.

After a five-month gap, I was back at work when I was five months pregnant and continued working till the eighth month. It was a freelance training assignment and took only few days in the month. It is always exhilarating to work. There is no joy compared to the joy of working if you are in the profession you like and enjoy what you do. I am a trainer and I really like my work.

I did not feel too tired in the class. I remembered my last pregnancy, 2005-2006. I had taken classes till just a week before the delivery. May 31st 2006 was my last working day before I went on my three months maternity leave and June 6th I had delivered the baby.

One morning, I woke up to a bad attack of muscle cramps in my right leg. It is the one thing I dread the most about being pregnant. I had severe muscle cramps during the third trimester in the last pregnancy.

You can feel your flesh in your shank moving up and hardening. Excruciating pain! And there is nothing you can do about it. Just endure the pain and wait for the flesh to "melt" again and the pain to subside. It was strange that this time, it happened so early and that too in the morning. Maybe the past few days of standing during the training had something to do with it.

I was 64 kilos now. I was 58 at three months. That makes it a six-kilo jump. I had gained the maximum between the fifth and sixth months. Suraj, my student, had remarked on Facebook: if I was 60 at six months, does that mean that I will be 80 at eight months? OMG! That was a scary thought.

CHAPTER XII

Incontinence And The 'Hard' Part

I suffered from incontinence. It started many years after my first delivery. Pregnancy and childbirth are some of the known causes of incontinence.

I had my first baby at the age of 29. I started realizing I had incontinence at the age of 37-38. Advancing age, lack of exercise and vaginal delivery - these three factors contributed to my problem.

A loud sneeze, a laugh and the dam would break, and I would find myself wet to my thighs. I started wearing sanitary napkins just to contain the water flow and not end up wetting my clothes in public. But even those were not enough, if I laughed a lot.

Doctor suggested a minor surgery to contract the muscles so I could hold in the bladder longer. I did not go for the surgery.

Quite embarrassing the problem of incontinence is. Can't tell anyone and can't keep it from anyone. We women are literally on high alert all the time, especially when outside.

The 'Hard' Part

Let me now tell you about the actual hard part of pregnancy. It literally is the 'hard' part of pregnancy – Constipation. Pregnant women suffer from it.

I drink hot water to ease things. I eat guava to help. Guava is great. Within an hour of eating one ripe fruit, you can feel your stomach rumbling. And when you sit in the restroom and things start moving, you thank your stars, the hot water, and the guava for the miracle. And profusely curse progesterone. Progesterone is the hormone that makes bowel movement a nightmare during pregnancy. It relaxes the muscles, slows the digestive tract and with the additional space taken up by the baby and the weight of it on your bladder, constipation, and a constant urge to urinate, are common side effects.

Sometimes, we have a counting ritual in our family.

Day 1 mummy didn't go ...

Day 2 mummy didn't go ...

Day 3 mummy didn't go ...

It is then officially declared a family crisis. Tanvi springs into action and makes hot water for me. And they both wait for the good news that I went today. I have even called Sathya in his office to tell him that today was a 'good day'.

This is one of the reasons some men avoid pregnancy like the plague. The constant torture of getting updates of your wife's toilet struggles is not something they signed up for when they married you. But he doesn't grumble. He is a sweetheart. He listens. 12 years of wedded misery does that to you.

We have another secret understanding in our family. If it's day two of mummy not going, then it means it is "launch" day. It is time for them to hide for cover or if they are within striking distance then at least, cover their ears. They joke that when mummy is 'stuck', it is 'blast' time for them. And if we are outside, I whisper to Sathya and ask him to cover for me by pretending he did it. And then he mock practices suitable facial expressions so that it looks convincing enough! And does a final nod that acknowledges that he was the one who let out the sound. Those expressions he makes, it makes me laugh just thinking of it now. Tanvi mock runs like there was a grenade that dropped directly on her.

The Third Trimester

CHAPTER XIII

Discomfort

I was twenty-nine weeks pregnant, that is seven months. It was the start of the third trimester. At seven months last time, I remember telling Babu I will abort the baby. Things were SO bad! But this time, I could not wait to hold my baby in my arms. Most importantly, I could not wait to hold him along with Tanvi and Sathya. I could not wait to see their faces. I could not wait to show them the little one hiding inside me all these months.

The baby is now in a posterior position which means the head is down and legs up, his back pressing hard against mine. His jabs are stronger, more frequent and all three of us have felt and seen the kicks – the skin bouncing up, the hard kicks, the movement of the limb from one point to another, the hardening of the stomach walls.

Seventh month also means frequent urination. So frequent that I was not able to hold in, even a drop. It means there is no position comfortable enough to sleep. I am constantly struggling to place my stomach and find it hard to sleep. That pushed me into a desperate purchase of a body pillow from Amazon. Two months to go before the baby comes. I want to sleep as much as I can through my third trimester. I didn't use a body pillow during Tanvi's pregnancy but back then, I didn't have a smartphone, didn't use the internet much and didn't even know such a thing existed.

Tossing and turning at night has been a real ordeal. Every time I roll over, I must lift the weight of the new package in me to the other side, place it gently there and try to sleep again. The stomach is all out and there is not enough space for the three of us together on the bed. I had read that sleeping on the left side is the best position to sleep in.

I forced Tanvi to sleep on her bed, in her room. She kicks in her sleep and takes up half of the bed, leaving me clutching my stomach and waking up in the middle of the night wanting to twist her arm! I have had to show her how much space my stomach needs now and somehow have made her to sleep separately.

But every fifth day of the week, our little lady, aged 11 years, comes crawling back, like a cockroach, stealthily slides between us, promises not to trouble me and again, takes up more than half the bed!

Earlier when I used to wake up in the morning or I had not eaten for a long time and my stomach was empty, I would feel so light in my womb that I would almost end up doubting if the baby was really there. Stomach would look so flat. Now my stomach was visibly bulging, permanently out. I was aware of something hard in my lower abdomen. Hardness that did not go away.

One major change was I completely stopped drinking tea. I was a tea addict. I needed my two cups without which, in the mornings, I could not eat breakfast and, in the evenings, worried myself into a headache. I was the kind of obsessive tea drinker who would not go to a hotel that did not serve tea with the breakfast. I had to have breakfast WITH the tea. But now, I could not stand the sight or smell of it. I did not even buy tea powder. Strange.

I was 29 when I had delivered Tanvi. I will be 41 when I deliver this baby. Childbirth is an excruciating experience. With Tanvi, the pain of the contractions was killing. I was screaming like a mad woman. At that point in time as the pain hits you every five minutes or so, all you want is for the hellish experience to end. I can understand why some women choose to go for the C-section. But even now my thoughts don't let me consider C-section as an option. This time too I want to try my two hundred percent for normal vaginal delivery.

One reason is faster recovery and hence lesser dependence on others. The other reason is the cost factor. At Lakshmi Maternity, which is not one of those fancy, branded, corporate show-biz kind of a hospital, the charges for normal versus Cesarean deliveries are Rs 40,000/- and Rs 80,000/- respectively. That's a straight jump. C-section costs twice as much as a normal delivery.

I had not observed and reacted with glee to the movements of the baby in Tanvi's pregnancy. This time, I was observant of every little change, every twitch, every kick, every pain, every progress. I was eating well. I was sleeping well. I had been walking at least four times a week for half an hour. I was happy. That was how I wanted my pregnancy to be. I had wished for it. I was ecstatic that God had made my wish come true. It seemed incredible at the time that I too was experiencing a happy pregnancy. I used to think I was not fortunate enough and had made my peace with it.

If I had not known the darkness of my first pregnancy, I would not have been able to enjoy the light of this one. Everything was in comparison to it. Everything was better in comparison to it. Not just my own daily routine or health but also the relationship that I shared with Sathya. There was a sea change.

Earlier, there was love but it was overshadowed by pain, stress, doubt, distrust, anxiety, and uncertainty. Now, there was a quiet assurance in everything we did. I was content because I was relaxed in the comfort of his care.

Men Just Don't Get It

Women feel so emotional at times. We cry for no obvious reason. This is especially true during pregnancy.

But men just don't get it.

Do they?

I have explained this phenomenon to Sathya. I have explained it to him like a nursery teacher explaining ABCD to a kindergartner. I have explained that all he had to do when I am emotional, is HUG me. NOTHING ELSE is required.

Your smart-ass comments? No, not required.

Your 'be practical' advice? No, not required.

Your problem-solving tips and suggestions? No, not required.

Also, don't open your mouth to drop any of your male-ego satisfying, 'I know it all' gyan.

JUST hug me.

If you must open your mouth, open it to make sounds like 'umm' 'hmm'. You might think it's not good enough. But trust me. A hug, accompanied by these sounds, will do it for most women when we are crying our hearts out. The hug reassures us that you are with us. The sounds reassure us that you have not zoned out and are listening to us.

Quite simple, isn't it? Apparently, NOT!

Twelve years of marriage and two pregnancies later, I still have not succeeded in making my otherwise intelligent husband understand this.

Here's what happened once.

One day in November, I completed a 5 day training program for Lakme and the very next day fell sick. By Sunday morning, I ran a temperature. My arms and legs were weak, eyes were burning. At the hospital, they took a urine test for the possibility of a urinary tract infection and put me on drips to bring down the temperature. Went home, took the prescribed tablets Dolo 650 (yuck) and Tracfree Cranberry Extract (yum). By Wednesday, felt much better. But that afternoon, I woke up from my nap with severe chills. My body was shivering like a leaf caught in a storm. Sathya was worried and rushed me to the hospital again. The physician asked us to do a urine culture.

While waiting in the hospital, I held his hand, showed him the women who had come with their mothers and, with tears in my eyes, told him how most women take their mothers' presence and help during their pregnancy for granted. They pour out their frustration, anger, and irritation at their mother. They never think that they should not speak rudely or in a harsh tone to their mother.

Would they do it to their mother-in-law? No. Never. Not even in their dreams. That woman would never understand. But mothers are understanding and bear your wrath. If I had my mother with me, perhaps I too would behave similarly.

But for me mother, husband, and friend all three are one person only - he. I told him please don't be angry with me if I behaved with him how other women behave with their mothers. And then I folded my fingers and planted a kiss on his cheek.

He was embarrassed by this public display of affection.

When we came home, my state of mind was still tipsy. I was imagining, how it would be, had my parents been alive, how Sathya was father, mother, husband, and friend to me. I started weeping and called out to him. Thrice. I called out to him thrice! He was with Tanvi and her friends in the hall. He kept asking from there 'what-what-what' but did not come.

Finally, exasperated, I screamed "COME and sit next to me".

He came and asked, "What?"

I said, "Sit here."

He complained, "No place to sit."

I shouted, "Make place and sit".

I asked for his hand, told him I wanted to hold it for a while.

He asked, "Which hand?"

Seriously man?

Anyways, I had held it for a while when he said, "I can't sit in this position for long time" and came and slept next to me.

My tears had just started pouring out when he said the dreaded words, "Don't cry. There is nothing to cry."

I wanted to cry, I wanted to unburden the weight of my emotions, I wanted to feel light.

I replied, calmly, "Yeah right. Thanks. You can go now."

Men and their 'flat like a tyre', 'detached like a monk', completely unemotional response to a totally emotional situation!

I was speechless.

The First Thing You Bought

Do you remember the first thing you bought for your child when he was still in your womb? I don't remember for Tanvi. I did not buy anything when I was pregnant with her.

Back then, I neither had the time nor the interest to do any shopping. On the day of the delivery, it was Sathya who had rushed to the nearest shop and bought few essential items for immediate use.

But for this baby, a night suit was the first thing we bought. It was in Big Bazaar, Hebbal. This was when I was five months pregnant. We were casually strolling across the aisles in BB and stopped at the section for kids. Sathya was very keen on shopping for 'something'. So, we picked it - just like that.

Frankly, the section for boys' apparel is so boring. Just t-shirts and pants. The section for girls' apparel is SO tempting. It will not be a wonder if you feel to have a baby girl just so that you can dress your baby in all those fancy clothes.

Once the first piece came home, the shopping bug bit me. I logged onto Amazon and picked up all random stuff including baby powder, soap, diaper, and a carrying bag. Tanvi was carrying the bag around as if the baby was already in it. Even while watching TV, she would hold it in her arms and cradle it.

I was onto my eighth month and we still did not know if it was going to be a boy or a girl, but we continued to pick up boy tees!

The Ninth Month

I had entered the ninth month of my pregnancy. When you know all of this is happening within you, you feel so fortunate. The baby is growing at an accelerated pace. I remember the doctor mentioning in the growth scan report that the baby was in Cephalic position and I had googled to check what cephalic meant.

Just few more days left for the vitamin tablets. Nine months of taking them every day!

There had been too much on my plate the past two months. We went house hunting. With my third trimester stomach, we had been to see so many houses, in so many areas, on all kinds of roads. We not only shifted house, we also went on a road trip to Gandikota, Belum Caves and Lepakshi in Andhra Pradesh, and then, planned the baby shower.

The check-up frequency is twice in a month now. We had been for the bimonthly checkup. After that, it would be once a week. I am 37 weeks pregnant at a consistent 64 kilos. All tests are normal. By week 37, the baby is supposedly as heavy as a cabbage. As there is not a lot of spcae left in the womb, the baby feels the need to get out.

By week 39, the baby is ready to come out. He is almost 3 kilos by now. He is at the point where his lungs are about to scream out and cry. As he drops into the birth canal, the head is in the shape of a cone.

I had a nagging sense the delivery was going to be sooner. Tanvi had come 17 days prior to the EDD. This time I felt the baby had descended, the weight was more, and I found it hard to walk and carry my stomach around. It was already so difficult to turn or roll over at night with the stomach that feels hard at places especially lower abdomen. Whenever I picked up something from the ground, I would pray "Please don't slip off my hand." Because if it slips, I could not bend again to pick it up and it might lie on the floor for days. Bending is something I just could not do anymore.

CHAPTER XIV

We Are In It Together

This time around, it felt good to have Sathya next to me in the scanning room. In the first pregnancy, he would always be outside the hospital, busy smoking with Nayan, his best friend. I would be alone, inside, going through the tests and scans. It felt like it was just my child. It was inside my body and I had to take care of it. I had to do everything that had to be done. He had nothing to do with it. It was not his priority. It was not inside him, after all. Why would he be bothered?

This time, it felt like we were in it together. That is the biggest affirmation a pregnant woman needs. She wants to feel reassured that it is truly "our" baby. She wants to know, in no uncertain terms, that whatever needs to be done for the baby, we will do it together. Small things, big things – it doesn't matter. We are in it together!

Unfortunately, most men don't get this part. They don't do this.

DURING the pregnancy, they remain detached from the things going around in their wife's world. Once the baby is in their arms, they might change into a completely different person. They might turn into a 100% involved and doting father. But DURING the nine months, when only the mother can feel the presence of the baby in her womb, the father is distant. I wish for all would-be fathers to be involved in this phase. It makes a lot of difference to the emotional well-being of the mother and ultimately the well-being of the unborn baby.

May be I get why the fathers do not feel much. The baby is still an illusion for them. They cannot see the baby. They cannot touch the baby. They cannot talk to the baby. There is no sensory experience at all for the father to connect with the baby that is in the mother's womb. The kicks start mid-pregnancy and though they could be strong for some, they mostly are sensations felt by the mother. The full intensity of that moment is lost on most fathers. He has no way of knowing the baby personally.

But the mother feels the baby alive inside her. The mother and the baby are breathing together, living together, hand in hand, one breath at a time, day in and day out, every single day till the day of the delivery. The father is physically removed from this experience.

He must learn to imagine. He must learn to empathize. He must learn to dream and create. And that is a lot of learning to be done, a lot of effort. It is easier to get on with life and wait for the baby to appear and then see how it goes from there.

If pride was not attached to "my sperm", "my blood", I wonder if most men would even be bothered with the whole childbearing and child-rearing experience. The thing that fosters attachment of the man with the unborn baby is the sense of pride that his bloodline will continue. He feels his look-alike will ensure his immortality. That is the overriding sentiment for most men.

I read that It takes one full year for recovery from pregnancy and delivery. Who knew that? Most of us plunge right back into the routine of life. Wemust. What choice do we have? I don't think most mothers, the world over, have the luxury to take it easy after the delivery, that too for a whole year.

CHAPTER XV

Sex During Pregnancy

Can you make love during pregnancy? It is a question on every couple's mind.

During Tanvi's pregnancy, our honeymoon period and my pregnancy collided. Almost the entire duration of the first year of the marriage, when most couples are still discovering the nuances of each other's bodies, I was carrying a baby inside me.

Doctors regularly warn against sex during the first and last trimester. But we were reckless. No one or nothing would stop us. I was already 3 months pregnant when we went to Hotel Ashoka for our first New Year's Party. It was my first New Year's Party EVER! We danced together like crazy. Post that party, we went to a friend's farmhouse and made out in our car. I did not remember I was pregnant. In the initial four-five months of the pregnancy, it kept slipping my mind.

Another time, eight months pregnant with a huge protruding belly, we had gone to attend his cousin Vasu's marriage in H.D Kote. We made out on the roof of the wedding hall. Raging hormones? You bet!

Is there a difference in the pleasure sensations? Is there a difference in your experience when you are newly married and now, when you are older? I think there is. When you are young and raw and new in your relationship, it is more of "fun" and “let's do it, anywhere and everywhere!" and "Hey, we never did it in this place or this corner or on this table!” The thrill that the fear of being caught generates, and not actually getting caught, is tempting and enticing.

Now, after many years of marriage, it truly is about the emotional connection. You love your man more because he loves the child growing inside you. You are beaming at the thought of bringing another life into this world. This new life is yours and it will come into your arms one day. That thought binds the couple in an embrace that is tender and most loving. There is no rush, no expectation in that hug. The hug endears you to each other. It becomes an expression of "I really like you" and "I am glad we are in this together". And the body, during pregnancy, is on high alert, extremely sensitive to touch. It tingles.

Should you do it during pregnancy? You should not. Doctors warn you against it. You should not do it if you have any sort of medical complications or if it is forced. Each body, each couple and each pregnancy is different.

Strangely, I have been comfortable during both the pregnancies. The frequency has reduced greatly the second time around. That is because of the long years of marriage and advancing age. But the intensity of sensation has increased. All thanks to the same long years of marriage and the added sensitivity triggered by pregnancy.

The doctor advised us to avoid it. I still laugh at the way she pointedly looked at Sathya as if he was some sex maniac! He did look like one that day, with the overgrown beard and the 126-kilo body. So, I can't blame her. Of course, we didn't heed the warning this time either!

Does it hurt the baby in the womb? It did not in my case. Also, it is scientifically proven that it doesn't. The baby is ensconced in a snug and safe environment.

Does it cause advanced labor? It did not in my case. But that doesn't mean you can indulge in a "Circus" performance. Is it more pleasurable during pregnancy? Yes, it is, at least initially, when your belly is still not so big, and you can still maneuver. Later, your belly becomes a big hindrance and you will end up laughing at the awkwardness of it all. Those are tender moments and relish them while you still can because you are not going to go down that road again.

Caring For The Newborn

Why does a woman do that to another woman? Didn't my mother-in-law deliver three kids? Doesshe not know the pain of hunger? Why was she punishing me? What had I ever done to her? During Rutvi's delivery, I wanted to be aware and in control of the situation I was going to find myself in. I did not want to be hungry ever again.

My thoughts often wandered to the topic of caring for the newborn baby. It is a thankless job. If you have a mother, you take it for granted that she will take care of the newborn.

Most mothers-in-law don't like to take care of the newborn baby of their son, and it is accepted. No one questions her or asks her to change her attitude. You are lucky if you have a mother-in-law who voluntarily and wholeheartedly comes forward to help with the baby.

My ex-colleague, who was in her 50's back in 2012, was very clear that she did not want to raise her only son's newborn. "Let them do it. Why should I? It is my turn and time to relax. I have a life of my own. Why should I sacrifice it and be a nanny, an unpaid one at that?" My own mother-in-law has no affinity towards children, not even her own. Expecting her to pitch in with her son's baby was too far-fetched.

Childrearing is a humongous task, time, and energy consuming, with seemingly endless chores. Only a mother-in-law who is extremely maternal or loves babies or loves her son a lot or is dependent on her son for food and shelter, would be willing to do it.

My mother-in-law was 42 when her eldest son, my husband, had got married. Sathya was 25 years old at the time. At 43, she had become a grandmother. And look at me, here I am at 40, pregnant with my second child. At 43, I will be running after a little one, who would still be wobbling! At what age will I become a grandmother?Is it a generational shift? Are women getting healthier and younger with each passing generation? Or because we are marrying later (me at 28, mother-in-law at 18), are we hanging in there longer? Has education and financial independence had a positive impact on women's fertility, longevity, and overall health?

Post Delivery Diet

Your body is exhausted by the stress of pregnancy and the enormous pain of labor. Your mind is numbed by the emotional upheaval and your heart is distressed. The bare minimum you need, at such a time, to function normally, is food.

In Tanvi's case, I was discharged from the hospital four days after the delivery. I was in a stupor at the time and don't have a strong memory of those four days spent in the hospital.

But an overwhelming sense of being hungry still haunts me, even after all these years. Why was I feeling hungry all the time in the hospital? Sathya was staying in his parents' house. He ate with the others at home.Why couldn't he eat with me? He would go home to eat a proper meal. He had gala time roaming around with friends and eating a king's banquet at home. He would get food for me from his house. I would be sent a small cup of rice with some 'tilisaar' (the water collected from boiling dal, without spices or vegetables). I vaguely remember eating plain bread for evening snacks. I used to be famished. I was breast feeding, recovering, recuperating AND hungry.

I had to speak to the doctor. I think I told her, "I am very hungry doctor. I am not getting food. They are saying it is not good to eat too much post-delivery". The doctor was surprised to hear it and asked Sathya to feed me well, to give as much as I wanted and a proper meal, not some 'tilisaar' shit.

CHAPTER XVI

The Arrival

Any Day Now

The due date was 9th February. I had completed 37 weeks as on 21st January. Any day now the baby should be here. The next few days were crucial.

I had strange feelings. I was closer to having the baby come out and I felt like holding on to it a little longer! Though there were still nineteen more days as per the EDD, each day was taking me closer to the D-day. I was feeling movements in my womb and knew that very soon I would not feel them anymore. I was acutely aware that this was my last chance at pregnancy and motherhood. This sensation, of this baby alive and kicking and breathing inside me - I felt truly blessed.

The kicks and baby's movements within me were so precious. I knew only a few days were left for it. This is it. No more. Only memories of this sweet time. I had been pregnant two times in my life but had relished the pregnancy only this time. With Tanvi, the tensions in my life – money, job, newly married life – were so pressing that I never got around to enjoying it or even remembering it. This time, God has been kind and fulfilled my longing. I had truly enjoyed this pregnancy. Loved myself, loved the bump. Loved the care and attention shown by Sathya.

Few more days left. The baby will be here. Don't know if it will be a boy or a girl. Don't know if we over fantasized about it being a boy. Nine months have passed. Now it feels like it went by fast.

Sometimes, I think, at age 50, in another decade, I must have a third baby.

We planned to go to a fish spa and as I got ready, I felt a leak. Half a small cup gushed out. We rushed to the hospital. While we were driving to the hospital, Sathya and Tan both were excited and looking forward to the baby.

Leela Rao did the glove test. Inserted her hand and said, "No, not yet ready". They put me on observation for an hour to see if the water had really broken. The maternity pad should be wet, she said. It was dry. We came home. False alarm.

Reminded me of the Steve Martin movie where both his wife and daughter are pregnant and due for labor at the same time and he goes nuts taking them on several such false alarm trips to the hospital. And when the labor hits, he has passed out on a couple of sleeping pills and he is the one who needs to be literally dragged and carried to the clinic.

Tanvi's was one of the shortest labors. At least that is what I have heard from many other mothers. Her due date was $23^{rd}$of June. On the $1^{st}$of June, her head was fixed. On the 6th the water broke. From the time I was taken to the operation theater to the actual delivery, it was all over in two hours. I have heard of labors that have lasted almost a day.

Don't know what is going to be my fate this time around. I hope Tanvi's little brother or sister is going to be as sweet and as much in a hurry to come out as she was!

Every day I was waiting and wondering when the baby will choose to make its appearance. The movements are still strong, and we can see the skin stretching, extending. Sometimes, we can feel and see the head sticking out and sometimes, the limbs. We can feel the hardness of the body inside.

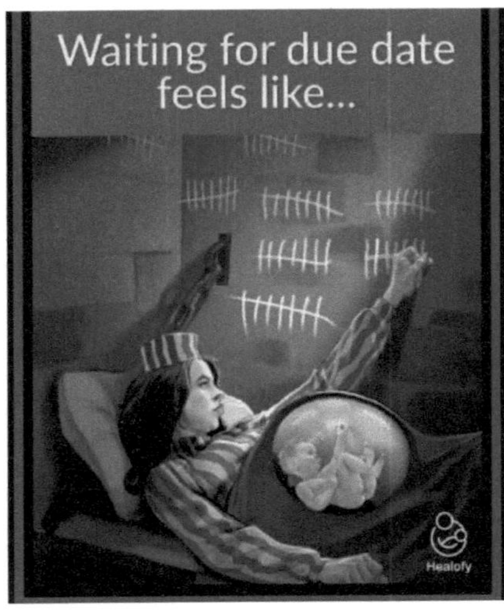

All I can do now it wait. Wait for him to choose his time and day. Today is 25thJan. I wish he chooses 28th Jan or 1stFebruary. Both are number 1 date. And sometimes, I just want him to come out right away. Enough carrying this heavy package around and struggling to sleep comfortably.

Last time, I was working full time.So, didn't even realize when the nine months had passed. Add to that, Tanvi came seventeen days early.

One night, woke up at 12:00 a. m and slept at 4:00 a.m. I was crying.

I was crying that the baby hadn't come out. I was desperate. Ninth month turned out to be the hardest. By now, I had experienced everything there is to experience in terms of pain, nausea, cramps, fatigue.

But this wait, this seemingly endless wait, this carrying around the baby, heavy stomach and the accompanying tiredness, this not knowing when the baby will come and not knowing why is the baby taking so long to come, this is really mind-numbingly painful.

The Arrival

6thFeb was our weekly doctor visit day.

Like the previous week, we had other plans after the hospital visit - maybe eat out or watch a movie or pick up Tanvi from school. Stuff like that.

My water had not broken. I did not have pain or contractions. Nothing. The assistant doctor did the routine BP and weight check. This was at 12:30 p.m.

After an hour, Dr. N came. She saw the due date, examined me and said, "You have opened. Get admitted. We will do it tomorrow”

I was surprised. "Wait! What? You mean I will have the baby tomorrow? The baby is here? I am ready? But...wait...tomorrow is 7th. My baby will be born on my mother’s DOB. And Sathya and his two brothers were also born on the 7th of their respective months and his mother too. 7this not a good date” I heard my mind rambling.

All I said aloud was, "Last time, the water had broken. It was normal delivery."

Immediately, the doctor said, "Ok. Then we will do it today."

I still don’t understand what happened there. If she first said that the delivery will be done the next day, why did she change it to the same day.

Suddenly, we were faced with the news of the baby for which we had been waiting for so long!

In the pre-labor room, in the bed next to mine, the woman was told, "Have to do Cesarean. Call your husband." In the bed to the far left, one family was already discussing about the Cesarean bomb that the doctor had dropped on them. Meanwhile, a nurse connected me to a machine to track my BP. Lying down on my back was painful, but the nurse insisted on it. I was sweating. I hadn't eaten anything since breakfast, and I was tired and famished. And then, I saw panic on her face. I don't know to this day if it was all staged. She called a doctor to check. She examined me and said, "We have to go for cesarean."

I was shocked. I screamed "NO! I will push the baby. I will have a normal delivery." But it was inside my head.

Out loud, I beseeched "I want to go for normal delivery. What happened?" She said the baby was face up, her fingers had touched the teeth/gum/mouth of the baby. We asked to speak to Dr. N.

She examined and announced, "The baby has come down but face up. Even if you push, we can't have a normal delivery because the baby will get stuck while coming out. We HAVE to go for Cesarean".

At 1:30, when she herself had examined, everything was fine. Half an hour later, things had taken a sudden turn! They didn't even sit us down and explain things or take us into confidence before dropping the C word.

I felt so helpless.

Sathya came in. They gave us a moment. We stared at each other. It was all happening so fast and I was in so much pain. I felt I had let him down. I felt I had burdened him with the additional cost of the operation. I had failed him. I was on the verge of crying. I still couldn't believe I had to go for a Cesarean. Me? No. No. I had done everything to deserve a normal delivery. I had walked so much! Everyday! Deserved! What a strange word! How does one deserve a normal delivery?

They took me to the operation theater. The anesthetist explained to me that the lower part of my body would be numb, not to worry. I sobbed, "I wanted normal delivery".

They laid me on the operating table. I looked around. There were three lady doctors and one male doctor. There were machines near my leg and a blue sheet was put in front of my face. I was talking. The doctors were talking. They were discussing about breakfast and lunch. I was going in and out of consciousness. There were bits I was aware of, there were bits I wasn't. Like I remember I kept talking about normal delivery even there, with the operating doctors.

Dr. N said, "It's okay. Now you have the experience of both". I was angry to hear that.

Another doctor said, "All babies enter the world face down. Her baby is looking up. Like looking at the sky, head held high."

I didn't want my baby to look up. Why didn't she look down and come?

At 3:16 p. m, heard the doctor say, "Female. You have a girl baby."

I don't remember hearing the first cries of the baby. I even asked the doctor, "Did my baby cry?" They said yes, she did. I wanted to see her, hold her. They said she is with the pediatrician - getting cleaned and checked. They were busy stitching me up. The operation was over. I must have entered the operating room around 2:30 and by 3:30 everything was done. Getting me ready for the procedure, the operation, the stitch up. Super-fast.

No wonder, doctors prefer C-sections. No hearing a woman's wails and waiting for hours in case of natural birth. And more money too.

CHAPTER XVII

The Delivery Day

I was put on a stretcher to be moved into the ward.

I lay there waiting to see the baby. Just then, for a fleeting moment, one of the doors to the labor room opened and I saw Sathya and Tanvi outside. They were waiting to see us. When I saw them, the first thing that came to my mind was, "My world."

Exactly those words! They really are my entire world. They are everything. They are all I have. And I have a lot. That image of them standing there, Tanvi waving at me, Sathya anxious to know if I was okay...that image is imprinted in my mind's eye. In that moment, I knew I had all I wanted - with or without the new baby. I was fulfilled, complete. The baby was a bonus!

I hadn't seen the baby yet and asked a nurse for her. They brought her. I couldn't get up. But I held her. Momentarily! So much for all those viral videos you see online of mothers weeping, kissing, clicking pics with newborn, baby smooching the mother's face and so on and so forth. Didn't happen. The nurse took her out to show her to Sathya and Tanvi.

I wondered if they were upset that it wasn't a boy. I felt sad for them. Tanvi had said she wanted a brother and Sathya wanted a son he could play cricket with and teach bike riding to. I had disappointed them. I felt sorry. As for me, I was so happy that she was healthy and perfectly fine. That was all that mattered. Especially after the fear of Down's Syndrome.

I can't believe I am saying this but on hindsight, I think Dr. Nishchitha was right. I had the experience of both cesarean and normal delivery. It opened my eyes. I was very skeptical of C-section deliveries. I used to think it was a way God was punishing the women for something. I thought it was a shortcut some women took to avoid the pain and have it easy. I thought if someone had to go for cesarean, it is because they were not healthy. Healthy women were blessed by God and had normal deliveries.

I was a complete idiot. I was a moron, an asshole. How could I think like that? I had no idea of the pain the surgery involved. But after I went through it because my baby was born through Brow Presentation (face is the first thing at the opening of the birth canal, not head) and I had no option but to say yes to a surgery, I realized that I was SO wrong.

In the case of a normal delivery, the pain is <u>during</u> the delivery. It could be for a couple of hours to sometimes a day. In the case of a C section, the pain is <u>after</u> the delivery. Even though the baby is out in a couple of minutes and there is no pain that the mother feels at THAT moment, the pain of the stitches and the back pain and the slow healing and the painful recovery is a long process. In one case, you suffer pain for a few hours but rest of your life, you will be fine. As in the case of Tanvi's delivery. In another case, you don't suffer pain in the beginning but suffer it throughout your life. Or at least, that's what people tell you about the lifelong pain.

I don't know about doing it all over again. I wouldn't!

People glorify pregnancy and motherhood. I can totally understand and empathize if a woman would rather adopt than go through all this.

The Best Day?

I remember reading this line somewhere:

"I may have hated the pain and I may forget it but the day I have given birth was the absolute best day of my life."

I don't agree. I don't think it was the best day of my life by any stretch of imagination. This line is just another way of glorifying the whole birthing process. I have delivered two babies. Both the days were MESSY, to say the least. Normal or C-section - it doesn't matter. You are a MESS.

Take a sneak verbal preview of what usually happens on the delivery day.

Doctors (yes, plural) stick their fingers into you. A nurse disrobes you. One staff puts a bed pan under you (in case of normal delivery) and asks you to relieve yourself so that you don't shit during the delivery (some still do). You can feel your stomach and large intestines emptying into that pan and then the staff takes that pan in front of you into the toilet and flushes it and you almost die of shame (if it's your first delivery).

Another staff comes and "cleans" you. Add to that, your madwoman like screams during the contractions and unbearable hunger, your body being paraded and handled most unceremoniously, and you cannot even protest. I could go on.

Point is - it is NOT a pretty sight.

In India, most hospitals do not allow the husbands into the labor rooms.I feel husbands should be allowed to see their wives in their WORST possible avatar and see if they still love her as much. Indian husbands have no idea what their wives go through, on the D-day, to give them their DNA, in flesh and blood, angelic and cherubic, wrapped beautifully in softness of cloth and skin.

And those videos that show the baby and the mother bonding - well, with both my babies (I delivered them in the same hospital, 12 years apart), the nurses took them away almost immediately to be weighed and cleaned and a hundred other things to be done like noting the time of birth etc. The bonding and the skin-to-skin contact that pregnancy websites emphasize so much on happened a few hours later in my case.

Face Presentation

Saw this word for the first time on my hospital discharge summary report.

No matter how much you read on the topic of pregnancy and birth when you are pregnant, there's always something you miss. Who knew my baby would choose to come into the world through an FP?

Statistics say only one out of 300 deliveries are FPs. Normally, a baby is born headfirst. The chin is bent towards the chest. But in an FP, the chin is stretched, the neck is extended backwards, as if the baby is looking up.

Brow Presentation and Face Presentation

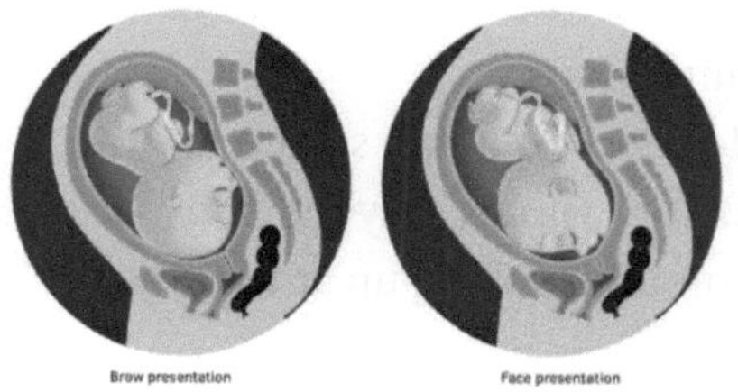

They say if an Face Presentation is mismanaged, there is the possibility of birth defects and skull trauma.

A million thanks to God and the doctors for ensuring my baby was delivered safely, that she was fine and did not suffer any pain or swelling of face or any other trauma.

Today, the more I read about FP and watch images or videos related to it, the more grateful I am for my baby's safe delivery. My C-section delivery apprehensions be damned! I have a healthy baby in my hands. That's what matters.

But on the day of the delivery and post that, I was really upset. I kept asking myself, and Sathya - why did our baby choose to come this way? Why couldn't she have not flexed her neck muscles? Why couldn't she have 'looked down', tucked her chin into her chest and come out like hundreds of other babies? I could have easily had a normal delivery. We could have saved money and post-delivery recovery time spent in the hospital. I had no complications, whatsoever, during my entire pregnancy nor on the day of the delivery. No pain or contractions or bleeding or high BP. Not even water discharge. Just the news that the baby will exit the womb today. Did the baby look up on the day of the delivery or at the exact moment of her entry into the world? When did she flex her neck? It certainly did not show up in any of the scan reports or during the weekly physical examinations.

I have decided to take solace in the words of the operating doctor who said, your baby has held her head high and is coming, looking up at the sky.

Afterword

So, should you go for a second child? You absolutely must. It makes the whole experience two-fold endearing.

If you have loved your first pregnancy, great. You will love the second one even more. If you have not loved your first pregnancy, no problem. You will love this one.

Yes, it does put a break on your career, health, and social life. Yes, it drains your finances. Yes, it does seem unending and exacts a heavy toll on your mind and body. But at the end of it all, it still is worth it. The bonds that grow within your family with the addition of the newest member is heart-warming. It is worth all the sleepless nights. It is worth the stretch marks and the belly fat.

I have felt greatly blessed. It is no less than a miracle to be pregnant at 40 and deliver a healthy child at 41. When you hear and see the number of couples who long for this happiness, when you hear of their struggles to have a child, the extent to which they are ready to go just to conceive once, you will only thank God for what you received without asking for it.

Conception is the universe's greatest miracles. Watch videos to realize just how difficult it is to fertilize the egg. A million sperms fighting off each other to penetrate one willing and eagerly waiting egg. The fertilized egg going through miraculous transformations to form into a human at the end of nine months is a thing of beauty.

If you have been pregnant without trying too hard, if you have been able to have a child without outside intervention and medical assistance of any sort, be thankful. It is a blessing.

Whenever you are besieged by doubts and are torn between career and kids, choose the kids. You can always choose career later. There will be plenty of time to choose work. And plenty of work to choose from.

Enjoy the joys of parenthood. Be grateful for the camaraderie between the siblings. Enjoy their playtime and their laughter. Enjoy the little things of pregnancy – the cravings, the aches, the growing belly. Everything seems precious and ephemeral. You know this is your last chance at being pregnant. Relive the moments one last time.

Everyone seems to be more involved in the process this time around and you appreciate their participation. The things you missed last time are in your life once again and you relish them. The baby's growth, first teeth, first words, first step – everything has an exaggerated sense of beauty to it. One thought constantly at the back of your mind is: This Is It! No more! This is one last time you would be enjoying these beautiful life moments and then you would be back to the strife and chaos of regular life.

The baby's smile, hug and sweet loving whispers mean so much to you now. When the baby showers her elder sister with warm kisses, you experience a warm, fuzzy feeling. You feel you have done and accomplished something in your life. This must be payback time from the universe. You are rewarded for your past good deeds with these moments of joy that you now get to see every day.

How This Book Came To Be

I had initially created a blog in 2012 to chronicle Tanvi's growing up years. It mostly had pictures of Tanvi from six months to five years old. Nothing else at all.

I could never, somehow, get around to updating the blog regularly. It could be because of a lack of time, lack of dedication or just plain laziness or a combination of all three and the blog stayed inactive and non-existent.

I planned to change that. It was time to breathe life into it! Thanks to Suzaan's suggestion, in 2017, I converted the blog to chronicle the journey of my second pregnancy and named it New Life New Journey. I wanted the blog to be exclusively regarding pregnancy, mostly for new moms or other pregnant women. It was going to be a journal of all the things we women experience during the nine months. Most of the content was going to be mundane, some explicit, some graphic and some cringe worthy. But then, so is pregnancy. It is all of it at different times. It is a bitter-sweet experience. It has its ups and downs.

Like the time I started "Conversations", I felt butterflies in my stomach. I was nervous and excited. If nothing else, I wanted to be able to blog right up to the ninth month. And if no one reads, I hoped, at least, my little ones will read it someday.

And today, the same blog has transformed itself into a book you are holding in your hands.

I hope you enjoyed reading this book as much as I enjoyed writing it for you. It is a heart to heart conversation between two mothers.

9 798885 215206

Printed by Libri Plureos GmbH in Hamburg,
Germany